#Spe...

Maj D.

This is a work of fiction. Any similarities to actual events, real people, living or dead, or to real locals are entirely coincidental. All references to real places are intended to give the novel a sense of reality and is used fictitiously.

This book was printed in the United States of America.

DEDICATION

This book is dedicated to my Beautiful Guardian Angel "Lyla Chantrelle". Mommy everything I do is for you. And I know you're very Delightful with my Accomplishments. Continue to watch over me, I love you beautiful lady. Kisses. Mwah.

TABLE OF CONTENTS

Different poems and a variety of Motivational and Inspirational Quotes in between each poem. .

ACKNOWLEDGMENTS

First, I want to Thank my Best Friend "King Jesus" for giving me the gift to create this Phenomenal Book for you guys. Also I would like to Thank my father Claude Dorismond for taking care of me and my sister after my mom passed away when I was just one years of age. Can't forget about my smart mouth sister Magdala Dorismond, I want to Thank her for always being tough on me when she felt that I needed it. Lastly, I want to Thank my beautiful amazing Godmother Tracey Martin for always being here for me, even when I felt like I didn't deserve it.

INTRODUCTION

Entering my second book #SpeakFreely. You should look forward to Poems, Inspirational and Motivational Quotes I've written. This book was created while going through many trials that tried to attack me. And tried to hold me back, from my destiny while sitting in the County Jail. Yet, God always come through for me. Hope you guys enjoy this book I created for you all.

JAIL

Jail is the worst place to be.
It's like losing all your privileges off the streets.
Guards telling you when to eat,
sleep and shit.
I wouldn't want this on,
No one
Not one bit.
Sometimes I wish I had
No time for some of the mess and shit I did.
Why do we let our feelings take over our strength?
Putting us in positions we never want to be in.
Jail have you so stressed and tensed.
I wish you well after your time inside the pin.
Now your best bet,
Is to never go back again.

GOOD PEOPLE ARE HARD TO FIND, SO WHEN YOU FIND SOMEONE GOOD. PLEASE DON'T WASTE THEIR TIME, TIME IS PRECIOUS AND CAN NOT BE TAKEN BACK.

NEVER ALLOW THE NEGATIVE FEEDBACK TO STOP YOU FROM DOING POSITIVE THINGS, LIKE FOLLWING YOUR DREAMS.

AREN'T YOU TIRED OF
MEETING NEW FRIENDS.
THEN THE FRIENDSHIP
ALWAYS END. TRUTH IS
PEOPLE ALWAYS PRETEND.
THAT'S WHY I CHOOSE GOD
AS MY FRIEND TIL THEE END.

IF YOU CAN ADMIT TO
YOURSELF YOU NEED TO CHANGE
AND IS WILLING TO CHANGE.
CHANGE WILL COME WITH
DETERMINATION AND FOCUS ON
THE NEW YOU. BELIEVE YOU CAN
CHANGE AND YOU WILL.

TIME FOR A CHANGE

I'm guilty of a lot of things,
Like things I cannot change.
Reacting to situations that cause no pain,
So why sometimes I'm busting my brain,
Screaming and yelling like it's all gone change.
Sometimes I wish some things can go away for change.
Damn sometimes living life becomes so lame,
Crying for help,
Like it's time for change.
Trying to build the courage to move forward without
going insane.
Man I wish life was a part of my domain,
I ain't gone lie I wish I had a heart like God,
Cause his love for us will make you wanna do a lot of
the right things.
Like calm your nerves and sit down for a change,
Make you wanna scream and shout and say I know that
was you God you came when you knew I shouldn't act a
certain way.
God that was you when I was on memory lane.
Lifting me up and showing me I deserve better than
this way,
I know it's time for a change,
Unless I'm gone continue being this way.

CAN'T COMPLAIN ON THE PAST,
THAT'S TIME THAT CAN'T BE
TAKEN BACK.

WHATEVER STOPS YOU
FROM GOING, IS WHAT
SHOULD GIVE YOU
STRENGTH. YOU CAN DO
WHATEVER YOU PUT YOUR
MIND TO.

BE STRONG, EVEN WHEN HARD
TIMES TRY MAKING YOU WEAK.

NOT ALL DAYS ARE THE SAME, REMEMBER THERE WILL BE SOME GOOD DAYS AND BAD ONES. NEVER LOSE SIGHT. TROUBLES DON'T LAST ALWAYS. SOON EVERYTHING WILL BE OKAY, JUST GOTTA KEEP THE FAITH.

STOP JUDGING THE BOOK BY IT'S COVER. UNTIL YOU OPEN IT AND READ IT.

POLICE BRUTALITY

Police brutality,
Look at the shit they did to me.
Walking down the street,
And they locked me up over some weed.
Four years and graduated from college with my Bachelor's
Degree.
To still feel like a victim to everything.
Told myself I can't be a part of the system of Law
Enforcement,
Too much shit been happening.
Man a lot of people end up dead.
The system ain't nothing but hell,
Instead of giving us a chance,
They lock us up and dance.
Thinking this shit funny,
Cause they have the authority to remove you off the
street without a chance.
Now I see how some people take the Law into their own
hands.
Shit.
The system don't give a damn.

THEY SEE YOUR SUCCESS, EVEN WHEN THEY DON'T HAVE THE COURAGE TO CONGRATULATE YOU.

BEST BLESSINGS IN LIFE, IS GETTING THROUGH THE DAY TO WAKE UP TO THE NEXT.

VISUALIZE AS IF IT WAS REALITY.

SOMETIMES THE MIND DOESN'T AGREE WITH THE HEART IN LIFE. NO MATTER WHICH ONE YOU CHOOSE, MAKE THE RIGHT DECISIONS EVEN IF ITS HARD OR IF IT HURTS.

YOU HAVE TO BELIEVE YOU CAN DO IT. AND IT CAN BE DONE. BELIEVE IN YOU.

I WANNA BE SO FOCUS, THAT I DON'T GET DISTRACTED AND LOSE MY VISION.

YOUNG DREAMERS

All young beautiful girls and boys deserve to live their
dreams,
No matter how hard they may seem.
It's starts from a dream,
Waking up to chase the unseen.
Never allow no one to crush what you can turn from a
Dream into Reality.
Anything possible,
So don't never think thee impossible.
Don't ever tell yourself No,
Cause you can accomplish more than you'll ever know.
You just gotta keep the Faith,
You know,
And be thee Impossible.
I believe you can do great,
Going down the road.
Never let the Rejections make your Dreams go away,
You'll be doing exactly what the devil wants.
So stand firm and never let go.
Until you reach all your Goals,
And being Happy with what you worked hard for.

THINKING TRYING TO UNDERSTAND AND LEARNING IS VERY IMPORTANT. THINKING POSITIVE, ENDURES POSITIVE ENERGY.

PICTURE YOURSELF IN YOUR FUTURE. THEN GO OUT AND ACCOMPLISH WHAT NEEDS TO BE DONE, TO BRING YOUR DREAMS INTO REALITY.

ALWAYS REMEMBER GOD KNOWS WHAT HE'S DOING, EVEN WHEN YOU CAN'T UNDERSTAND THE PROCESS.

GOD INCLINED ALL YOUR TALENT INSIDE OF YOU, SO THAT YOU CAN GO OUT AND ACCOMPLISH THEM.

GOD SEES YOUR HARD WORK AND DEDICATION. YOUR EFFORT IS NEVER GOING UNNOTICE.

HARD WORK, DEDICATION AND EFFORT EQUALS TO SUCCESS.

SEASON

Even when I try my best to be Humble,
I still turn around and Stumble.
Why is it that to be Humble,
We have to always Fumble.
Just wish it was another way,
So we can always have a good day.
Seems like even when we Pray,
Our days always go Astray.
Sometimes my mind go Blank,
It be so hard for me to think.
Not always trying to drink,
But I be about to go insane.
From all the things I'm thinking,
Sometimes it be for no Reason,
But I understand it be just for the Season.
So I try to forget the Season,
And move on without a Reason.

WAKE UP EVERY MORNING WITH THE MINDSET OF (I GOT TO GET IT). BRING YOUR DREAMS INTO REALITY.

DETERMINATION IS THE KEY TO SUCCEED. STAY DETERMINED.

JUST KEEP YOUR EYES ON THE PRIZE AND FOCUS ON RECEIVING YOUR TREASURE. WORK HARD. YOU SHALL PREVAIL.

LET YOUR DRIVE, DESIRE AND YOUR DETERMINATION LEAD YOU TO ACCOMPLISH EVERY DREAM.

BE WHO YOU ARE AND OVERCOME WHAT YOU FEAR.

THINGS GO WRONG. BUT IT'S UP TO YOU TO HOLD ON TO WHAT HAPPENED IN THE PAST, A FEW MINUTES AGO OR EVEN YESTERDAY. DON'T LET NOTHING STEAL YOUR PEACE. TROUBLES DON'T LAST ALWAYS.

UNGODLY PEOPLE

Ungodly people,
Always trying to harm others,
By doing things that's evil.
Like using them,
And telling them that the God they serve is equal.
But how can you serve God,
By doing the things you do.
That's not from God,
Are you that freaking evil.
Stop using God to con others,
Cause what you doing is clearly see through.
God don't indulge into wrong doings,
That's done to his people.
He protect the ones he loves,
And put those to shame who mistreat you,
Cause in his eyes they are not equal.
He is Faithful to those who don't condone into evil.
Ungodly people can't harm Gods servants or his people.

DON'T STAY DOWN. NEVER GIVE UP, UNTIL YOU REACH THE TOP.

WAKE UP, PRAY, THEN GO GET IT. FOLLOW YOUR DREAMS, NO MATTER HOW HARD THEY MAY SEEM.

BE WHO YOU ARE. YOU WERE MADE TO BE UNIQUE, SO BE YOU.

DON'T DREAM TO LONG. OWN IT, LIVE IT. IT'S ALREADY YOURS. CHASE IT.

IT'S YOUR LIFE, SO LIVE IT. BE HAPPY, MAKE MISTAKES AND LEARN FROM THEM. THEN MOVE FORWARD.

BEING DIFFERENT IS VERY UNIQUE. I'M GLAD TO BE DIFFERENT, I'M PROUD TO BE ME.

FAITH WITHOUT BELIEVE

What's Faith without Believe?
Believing in the word of God.
Will lead you to a lot of beautiful things.
Things we cannot see,
Not like the ocean and sea.
Jesus overcomes all things.
Like the apples falling from the trees.
Imagine doing good deeds,
For people that's in need.
God rewards you with things,
You can Praise on the scene.
To bring people to his kingdom,
And they would Believe in all things,
That's sent from Heaven.
Like his Kings.
Having Faith is not seen,
But you have to be strong to endure the good things.
God has prepared for you.
Believe in him,
And you will witness all the great things.
What's Faith without Believe?
It's like Satan doing evil wrong things.
Seek God,
And you will Succeed.

I REMEMBER WHEN I DOUBT MYSELF. TIL I PUT MY FEAR ASIDE AND STEPPED OUT ON FAITH.WITHIN SEVEN MONTHS I'VE ACCOMPLISHED A LOT. I CAN'T THANK GOD ENOUGH FOR GIVING ME THE STRENGTH I HAVE NOW THROUGH ALL THE REJECTION I'VE BEEN THROUGH IN MY LIFE.

WE ALL ARE AMAZING INDIVIDUALS. EMBRACE WHO YOU ARE.

THE BEST GIFT IS LIFE.
SECOND BEST IS LIVING.

HOPE CONQUERS FEAR.
ROAR AND OVERCOME WHAT
YOU FEAR. YOU ARE STRONG.

STOP PRETENDING TO BE
SOMETHING YOU ARE NOT. AND
START FOCUSING ON WHO YOU
ARE DESTINED TO BE.

BLESSINGS

Living life without lessons.
How can you get your blessings?
Life takes you in so many different directions.
After a while you start to see God progressing.
And all the stressing go in different directions.
So you can start manifesting.
Be strong no matter how hard it starts to getting.
Without all the shaking and beating,
You won't be able to accept all your blessings.
So stop all the stressing,
And allow God to direct you to all your blessings.
Then you will be able to tell the world,
It was God that you accepted.
And he directed you to all your blessings.

BELIEVE THAT YOU CAN AND YOU WILL. IT'S ALL UP TO YOU. YOU GOT THIS. TRUST YOURSELF.

PRIDE TAKES AWAY A LOT OF YOUR PEACE. EVEN THROUGH THE WORST SITUATIONS, DON'T ALLOW YOURSELF TO MISS YOUR BLESSINGS, FROM WHAT HAS ALREADY BEEN DONE. BE STRONG, HOLD ON. YOUR TIME SOON WILL COME ALONG.

DRAMA IS FOR LOSERS.

DON'T LET YESTERDAY'S PROBLEM, TODAY'S ISSUES. LET IT GO. YOU DESERVE PEACE.

LIVING LIFE, NEVER WAS MEANT TO BE EASY. THINGS WILL GET BETTER. STAY STRONG.

BE FAITHFUL

Be Faithful to God,
As he is Faithful to you.
Because of God,
We are here on this Earth today.
I know you may feel anger and hurt,
But in due time all the bad things will go away.
If you continue to Pray and Believe in our Lord God
always.
God is Faithful to us through our sinful ways.
Only if you surrender,
You will receive all the blessings that you missed
yesterday and other days.
God is Faithful,
Believe and he will make a way.
Be patient and you will see many better days.
Be Faithful to God,
And you will live a good life today,
Tomorrow and many more days.

IF YOU CAN DREAM IT, YOU COULD ACHIEVE IT. GO FOR IT, IT'S ALREADY YOURS.

CHASE YOUR DREAMS, NO MATTER HOW HARD THEY MAY SEEM. YOU CAN DO IT.

THE ONLY WAY YOU GONE GET WHAT YOU WANT, IS BY GOING AFTER WHAT IT IS. YOU ARE THE ONLY ONE THAT CAN BRING YOUR VISION TO REALITY.

STOP DOUBTING YOURSELF. ANYTHING CAN BE DONE, ITS ALL UP TO YOU.

REMEMBER YOU DON'T NEED NO SUPPORT. BE YOUR OWN SUPPORT AND BELIEVE IN YOURSELF.

NOBODY WANNA SEE YOU UP, SO THEY DOWN YOU WHEN THEY CAN. DON'T FEED INTO IT, UNLESS ITS ABOUT MONEY.

GIVE ME STRENGTH LORD

Judge me from yesterdays,
Only because it wasn't a perfect day.
Making mistakes can only bring,
Brighter tomorrows.
So why every time I pray,
Sometimes they always go astray.
Am I wrong for feeling torn,
Or am I supposed to continue to pray.
Looking for a better tomorrow,
But lately my Faith is flowing away.
God I bow my head down,
Asking you to lead my way.
Are you listening to my prayers,
Or should I continue to believe in you.
In every way.

CHANGES CAN BE DONE. BUT IT STARTS WITH YOU. ANYTHING IS POSSIBLE.

PRAY FOR PEACE, IF YOU DON'T ALREADY HAVE IT. PEACE BRINGS JOY, BEST FEELING.

STOP FOLLOWING AND START LEADING. BE THE BOSS, AND DON'T GET BOSSED AROUND.

YOUR DREAMS ONLY GOES AS
FAR AS YOU TAKE THEM. IF
YOU WANT IT, GO GET IT.

IT TAKES A TEAM TO BUILD A
VILLAGE. IT'S A LOT OF
VILLAGES ON THE WAY. AND
WE'RE NEXT UP,
IF WE TAKE OFF. TAKE WHAT'S
YOURS.

IF YOU CAN HELP SOMEONE
ELSE ACCOMPLISH THEIR
DREAMS, YOU ARE A HERO.

LORD SAVE ME

Times like this,
I just want to quit.
Quit everything,
Because nothing's going right.
I've been putting up a fight,
And sometimes I can't sleep at night.
Wondering why,
I'm always going through bad times.
Crying for help,
And I just want to give up on myself.
I know I was born alone,
So I gotta continue being strong.
It's my life to live,
So I gotta give myself the strength to surrender
and rethink.
Think before I speak,
And not get upset for anything.
Asking myself how can I have peace when I overthink
everything.
I need to relax my mind,
And continue trying to shine.
Understanding that the world don't revolve around me,
So I have to stop and think.
Think of others feelings and not just mine.
Learning to give it some time,
And maybe things can unwind.

I believe in me,
So I will be giving myself the benefit of the doubt,
To change my life around.

BELIEVE YOU CAN DO ANYTHING.
THEN DO IT.

THINK POSITIVE, REACT
POSITIVE AND YOUR
OUTCOME WILL BE POSITIVE.

DREAM BIG.

IF YOU HAVE PASSION FOR SOMETHING. UNDERSTAND THAT GOD INCLINED THAT INSIDE OF YOU, FOR YOU TO PURSUE WHATEVER YOU HAVE PASSION FOR. DON'T BE AFRAID TO CHASE YOUR DREAMS. GOD IS RIGHT THERE WITH YOU.

DARKNESS

Crying day and night,
Cause things in my life just ain't right.
Been putting up a fight.
Now I'm just ready give up tonight.
I'm so tired of hearing,
Everything's gone be alright.
But when is that time,
So I can have peace inside.
Peace is all I want,
But all I get is darkness day and night.
It's said that the storm don't last long,
But what's long if I don't have nothing left inside me to
Put up another fight.
I just wanted everything in my life,
To make it without a fight.
I guess I'm asking for too much,
Right.

WE ARE ALL HUMANS. WE WILL HAVE DOUBTS. BUT DON'T LET THOSE DOUBTS TURN YOUR VISION AWAY. STAND STRONG IN WHAT YOU BELIEVE AND WHAT YOU WANT TO ACHIEVE. WE ALL ARE DESTINED FOR GREATNESS.

LIVE IN PEACE AND LET GO NEGATIVITY.

YOUR PASSION WAS
GIVING TO YOU BY GOD.
STRIVE TO YOUR DESTINY
AND ACCOMPLISH
EVERYTHING YOU DREAM
OF. ANYTHING IS
POSSIBLE, JUST BELIEVE
IN YOURSELF LIKE GOD
BELIEVE'S IN YOU.

BE DETERMINED AND
STAY FOCUSED.

RUN AWAY

Sometimes I wish I can run away.
Run away from my thoughts.
The doubt,
Doubts about life.
How life changes dramatically.
Thinking about?
Will my life be how I dreamed it would to be.
Or is it just a dreams,
Cause I keep having imperfection moments,
Where I don't know where I'm going.
Or is there something God is showing me.
Questioning myself asking,
Will I ever be that person I dream of.
Looking at the sky above,
Asking the Lord to just give me a hug,
Screaming towards the sky asking God can he humble me.
Screaming Lord why,
Cause all the doubt on my mind.
Thinking sometimes will I ever be so kind.
Ion want my vision to make me think it's all a lie.
Cause the devil comes in disguise.
Trying to turn me towards his lies,
But deep down inside.
I already know it's a lie,
So I gotta force my mind to look away at all the times.
But yet I'm so depress,
Like a wolf grabbing my chest.
Wondering if I deserve the things that I want in life.

DON'T HIDE WHO YOU ARE SO
OTHERS CAN BE PLEASED. BE
YOU AT ALL TIMES AND LIVE
COMFORTABLY AS YOURSELF.

NO RESULTS, TRY HARDER.
DON'T QUIT. QUITTERS
NEVER SEE THE SUN SHINE.

STAY STRONG. STORMS DON'T
LAST LONG. YOU WILL BE
VICTORIOUS, KEEP BELIEVING.

STOP BEING HARD ON YOURSELF. DIFFICULT SITUATIONS WILL COME. BUT YOU HAVE TO BE STRONG AND DON'T LET IT KEEP YOU DOWN. STICK YOUR CHIN UP AND MOVE FORWARD. IT'LL ALL BE WORTH IT, BUT FIRST YOU GOTTA BELIEVE.

BEAUTIFUL FUTURE

Days ahead are meant to be beautiful,
But it starts with what's within you.
Don't worry about your yesterday's,
Just focus on your tomorrows.
You may not be proud of what you've done in your past.
Look at it,
And try to never go back.
Thinking of what you've done in your past,
Will only get in the way of what's ahead.
Don't worry about what's ahead,
Just do right,
Get on the right track,
And everything will fall in place,
The past will be erased.
Just continue to Pray and keep the Faith.
Then you will never have to look back.

FIRST STEP IS TO BELIEVE YOU
CAN DO IT. THEN DO IT.
FOLLOW EVERY DREAM AND
BRING IT TO REALITY.

NO MATTER WHAT YOU ARE
GOING THROUGH RIGHT
NOW. TODAY IS THE DAY
FOR YOU TO REJOICE AND BE
THANKFUL. EVERYTHING
WILL BE OKAY. YOU ARE
STRONG INDIVIDUAL.

LEVEL UP. NO MATTER HOW LONG THE PROCESS IS. EVENTUALLY THINGS WILL GET BETTER IF YOU DON'T GIVE UP.

KEEP PRAYING. KEEP WISHING AND MOST OF ALL KEEP THE FAITH.

MOTIVATION

Motivate yourself,
No need to get Validation from no one else.
Motivation,
Inspiration,
Preparation,
Is what you need to move through
Frustrations.
Lean towards the stars,
No matter how far you are.

TO BE EXCELLENT, YOU GOTTA
GO THROUGH THE LESSONS. SO
YOU CAN BE A PROFESSION AND
GAIN ALL YOUR BLESSINGS.

WHAT'S LOSING. WHEN YOUR
ONLY FOCUSING IS
WINNING.

AS LONG AS YOU LIKE
IT. FORGET WHO
DOESN'T. BE YOURSELF
AND BETTER YOURSELF.

TO HAVE PEACE
YOU HAVE TO LEAVE
BEHIND THE THINGS
THAT BLOCKS IT.

JUST ME

Never had real love around me.
Always been the black sheep of my family.
Literally nobody understands me,
Sometimes I feel like this not where I'm supposed to be.
I keep asking God to guide me,
But I'm always feelings so lonely.

THE HARDEST WE TRY, THE
HARDER IT GETS. BUT YOU
GOTTA BE STRONG. THINGS
WONT BE EASY BUT IT WILL
PASS. KEEP PUSHING.

I MAY NOT UNDERSTAND THE
PROCESS RIGHT NOW, BUT I
DO BELIEVE THE OUTCOME IS
GOING TO BE BEAUTIFUL. I
TRUST YOU LORD.

LESSONS INTO BLESSINGS

Living life without lessons.
How can you get your Blessings?
Life takes you in so many different directions.
After a while you start to see God progressing.
And all the stressing go in different directions.
So you can start manifesting.
Be strong no matter how hard it starts to getting.
Without all the shaking and beating,
You won't be able to accept all you Blessings.
So stop all the stressing,
And allow God to direct you to all your Blessings.
Then you will be able to tell the world,
It was God that you accepted.
And he direct you to all you Blessings.

YESTERSAY HAS PASSED SOMETHING WE CAN'T BRING BACK. FOCUS ON WHAT'S AHEAD.

SOMETIMES IT'S BEST THAT YOU WALK ALONE. IT'S NOT LONELINESS, IT'S JUST TIME TO FOCUS ON WHAT'S IMPORTANT FOR YOUR FUTURE.

THIS IS NOT THE END. I SEE MORE, I WANT MORE AND I WILL GET MORE.
#DETERMINED

FOCUS ON WHAT YOU WANT FOR YOUR FUTURE. LET THAT BE THE FOCUS OF YOUR LIFE.

PLAN IT OUT. THEN STEP OUT ON FAITH AND MAKE IT HAPPEN.

STOP PROCASTINATING AND START PARTICIPATING IN WHAT YOU ARE TRYING TO ACCUMULATE.

YOU LIED

I won't even lie,
My heart got broken for the last time.
You can see the tears in my eyes,
I just couldn't just not break down.
I thought it was love between you and I,
But look how things have come to an end.
You promised me that you will be by my side,
But I see you sat there and lied to my face.
This pain I'm feeling can't be erased,
I believed you when you told me through thick
and thin.
Now you got me wondering was this just a
faze.
I'm so dazed,
The promises you made,
Lied right to my face.
Now I can't believe not a word you say.

STOP THINKING YOU
CAN'T. AND GO OUT THERE
LIKE YOU CAN. IT'S OAKY
TO HAVE FEAR, AS LONG AS
YOU FACE THEM. YOU CAN
DO IT. I BELIEVE IN YOU.

STOP WASTING TIME AND
START MAKING CHANGES.
IT'S ALL UP TO YOU.

YOU HAVE TO PICTURE YOURSELF IN THE POSITION AND IMAGE YOU DREAM OF. THEN GRAB IT.

DON'T TURN AWAY FROM THINGS THAT'S RIGHT THERE IN YOUR FACE. AWAITING FOR YOU TO TAKE THE NEXT STEP. DON'T BE AFRAID. FOLLOW YOUR HEART, FOLLOW YOUR PASSION AND MOSTLY FOLLOW YOUR DREAMS.

CRIED OUT

Girl I'm pouring my heart out to you,
Not knowing what else for me to do.
I remember when we use to stick like glue,
Now I don't have a clue.
It used to be me and you,
Now we're growing apart like there's no tomorrow.
Can you hear my heart,
I'm all cried out.

RELEASE THE PAST AND INHALE THE FUTURE.

NO MATTER WHAT YOU ARE GOING THROUGH RIGHT NOW. UNDERSTAND THAT TROUBLES DON'T LAST ALWAYS. EVERYTHING WILL EVENTUALLY BE OKAY. YOU WERE BORN A STAR.

YOU EITHER WIN OR LOSE. LOSING ISN'T A OPTION WHEN YOUR PUSHING YOURSELF TO WIN.

SOMETIMES YOU NEED TIME TO YOURSELF. GIVES YOU TIME TO EVALUATE YOUR THOUGHTS AND FOCUS ON YOUR NEEDS. TAKE A COUPLE OF MINUTES AND HAVE SOME ME TIME INDEED.

EVERYTHING SHALL PASS AND IT ALWAYS DOES. CAN'T LIVE THE SAME BAD DAYS FOREVER, THERE'S A TOMORROW.

A PAIN THAT WILL NEVER GO AWAY

Thinking about my past,
Has me thinking of all the things I've been through.
Struggling through the pain,
That just seem to never go away.
Sometimes I ask my myself,
Why my life is so much hell.
Being so Rebellious,
And never listening to the ones who tried to help.
Honestly,
I can't say they tried to help,
Cause I always end up in hell.
Lonely,
Lost,
And so confused on how life supposed to help.
Help me get through the pain,
I felt when I cried out for God's help
Sometimes I
go insane,
Cause the death of my mother's pain.
And I still can't understand.
I try my best to gain the strength,
To wash away my pain.
But that's a pain I know,
That will follow me to my dying days.

YESTERSDAY HAS PAST, YOUR FUTURE LIES AHEAD. AND DON'T YOU NEVER FORGET THAT.

GO AFTER EVERYTHING YOU HAVE PASSION FOR, EVEN IF YOU DON'T KNOW HOW TO DO IT. ANYHTING IS POSSIBLE AND DREAMS DO COME TRUE.

I'M NEVER GIVING UP AND I MEAN THAT.

YOU EVER GET DRESS AND LOOK AT YOURSELF AND BE LIKE DAMN I'M FLY. I LOOK GOOD AS HELL EVEN IF NOBODY ELSE THINKS I DO. #LOVEWHOYOUARE

BE THE HERO OF YOUR OWN VISION. BELIEVE YOU CAN DO ANYTHING. AND BRING YOUR DREAMS INTO REALITY.

PLAN, FOCUS, THEN REACT.

SAFE AND WARM

Lord keep me safe and warm,
I have been going through so much troubles through the
storms.
My rainy days has gotten totally norm,
Lord can you help me to stay strong,
I cannot do it on my own.
Leaning on you,
Is where I belong.
God you helped me for so long,
And I appreciate you,
For what you've done.
So continues to keep me safe and warm.

GOTTA TRUST THE PROCESS.
FAILURE WILL OCCUR,
REJECTION WILL TOO. BUT YOU
CAN'T GIVE UP. THE OUTCOME
WILL BE BEAUTIFUL BUT IT'S
ALL UP TO YOU. IT'S COMING.

DO SOMETHING ABOUT IT,
THEN THE RIGHT THINGS
WILL HAPPEN.

EVERYDAY IS NOT THE SAME, SO
DON'T EXPECT THINGS NOT TO
CHANGE.

BE YOUR OWN HERO. BELIEVE IN YOURSELF. DON'T NEVER GIVE UP ON YOUR DREAMS.

YOU ARE THE ONLY ONE THAT CAN STOP YOUR DREAMS FROM BEING YOUR REALITY. DREAM BIG, REACT BIGGER.

FAILURE EQUALS TO SUCCESS. DON'T BE AFRAID TO FAIL. FAILURE HELPS YOU TO SUCCEED.

LORD HELP ME PLEASE

In times of need,
I sometimes drop down on my knees.
Begging God please to take me out of my misery.
Misery of all the trials that have let me down.
Asking you Lord can you Turn my frown upside down,
crying and looking around.
Notice that there's no 'one around that can help me out.
But I say out loud,
Lord don't forget I am your child.
I'm ready to bow down in front of you,
so I can be okay instead of being down.

DON'T RUSH THE PROCESS.
SOMETIMES IT'S GOOD TO TAKE
BABY STEPS. DREAM BIG. START
SMALL.

STAY IN YOUR OWN LANE,
DON'T LOSE FOCUS DURING
THE JOURNEY.

REJECTIONS SHOULDN'T KEEP
YOU FROM PROGRESSING.

THERE'S SO MUCH ROOM
INSIDE OF YOU FOR CHANGE,
PROGRESS AND SUCCESS.

THERE'S NO SPECIFIC WAY TO
BE. BE YOURSELF AND ENJOY IT.
FORGET HOW THE NAYSAYERS
FEEL. JUST BE YOU AND BE
GREAT AT BEING YOURSELF.

KNOW WHAT YOU WANT TO
DO AND DO WHAT YOU HAVE
TOO, TO GET IT DONE.

FOREVER MY LADY

Your forever my lady,
Will be forever my baby.
When I think about life,
I think about you like crazy.
When my nights get dark,
I think about you daily.
Who would have thought you would be my baby.
I go to sleep thinking about you in my dreams
And when I wake up it be the same thing.
Your smile makes me go crazy,
I can't lose you,
My whole life I'll be crying like a big baby.
I swear I can't see myself without my baby.
Them sweet talks we have turns me on like crazy.
Girl don't you know you will forever by my lady.

I LOVE MAKING MISTAKES. BECAUSE I LEARN FROM THEM.

I TRY MY BEST TO UNDERSTAND BY SEEKING KNOWLEDGE.

ITS OKAY TO START SMALL. AS LONG AS YOUR STARTING. BABY STEPS ARE GREAT.

YESTERDAY'S PROBLEM HAS PASSED. NO NEED TO LOOK BACK. TODAY IS A NEW DAY FOR IMPROVEMENT AND NOT FEELING IRRELEVANT. YOU WILL PREVAIL.

LIFE IS BEAUTIFUL. ONCE YOU SEEK YOUR DESTINY, YOU'LL SEE THE BEAUTY OF IT. EVERYONE DESERVES TO BE GENUINELY HAPPY AND LIVE THE LIFE THEY REALLY WANT. CHOOSE HAPPINESS.

MOVE PASS THE PAST

You worried about yesterday,
When that day has past.
Today is a new day,
So work towards something that will always last.
You have a chance to fulfill every dream.
But the Dream is something you should want to bring into
Reality.
Where you can see everything you did,
To get towards that shining star that you are.
Don't be afraid of the naysays,
Rejections or the confusions that always have your mind
Racing.
Keep chasing the pavements of your dreams.
Walk,
Crawl,
But never give up at all.
Reach towards the stars,
That's when you know your rode was hard,
But finishing up the trip will make it all worth it.
Moving through the storm when everything don't feel
Norm at all.
Crying out your heart,
Cause you wanna be a part of the change you wanna see.
Don't keep dreaming,
Work hard towards the unseen,
So you can see yourself on the Big TV screen.

UNDERSTAND THAT CHANGE
DOESN'T HAPPEN
OVERNIGHT.THROUGH THE
MIDST, TRY NOT TO PUT UP
A FIST.

LIVE YOUR LIFE HOW YOU WANT
TOO AND STOP CARING HOW
PEOPLE JUDGE YOU. FORGET
THEM AND FOCUS MORE ON
YOU.

DON'T RUSH THE PROCESS.
BE PATIENT AND TRUST THE
PROCESS.

I'VE OVERCAME SO
MANY OBSTACLES. A
LOT OF HARD ONES AT
THAT, BUT THROUGH
IT ALL I SURVIVED,
I'M ALIVE AND SO
BLESSED.

MY DESTINY

My gift is what you have given me.
I didn't ask you for nothing.
But guide me into my destiny.
If my destiny pertains writing what's within
me.
Then that's what it shall be.
You have given me words I can barely
pronounce with good literately.
But I still write and speak them literally.
Writing my thoughts to express my feelings and
what I do see,
I know now this is my destiny.
I know how I see what I speak freely,
not expecting anyone to understand my vision
but me.
You don't understand me or the words I
Speak, again this my destiny.
Should I express myself to make them in the
Outside world to understand me.
But Lord,
you make me understand I don't need nobody
But my king daily.
Providing me to speak freely,
I understand they will never understand my
words verbally.
So I continue to use these words you have
given me,
So I can show the world this what you gave
me.

You gave me a chance to write freely.
So I speak my mind freely.
This gift as a poet,
Writer and author really fits me.
That's why I'm thanking you tremendously.

STOP THINKING ABOUT THE QUALIFICATIONS YOU DON'T HAVE. AND WORK WITH WHAT'S RIGHT IN FRONT OF YOU "YOURSELF". HUSTLE, IT'LL COME TOGETHER IN THE END. BELIEVE IN YOURSELF AND KEEP PUSHING.

FOLLOW YOUR DREAMS NO MATTER HOW HARD THEY MAY SEEM. BELIEVE IN YOURSELF. KNOW THAT YOU CAN ACCOMPLISH EVERYTHING.

BELIEVE IN YOURSELF. IT'LL TAKE YOU SO FAR. REMEMBER ANYTHING IS POSSIBLE.

YOUR PRAYERS WILL BE ANSWERED. CONTINUE PRAYING, WISHING AND HOPING.

YOUR ALIVE, NOW YOU HAVE TO LIVE.

STAND STRONG

Discouragement is just so easy,
Especially when I can't see what God is really trying to
show me.
Storms have my mind pressed,
I'm so ready to get out this darkness mess.
Lord can you hear my cry,
I'm tired of feeling like my whole life is on the line.
I can't do this on my own,
So my Faith is how I move along.
I won't be discouraged through the storm,
Because you are the reason my life goes on.

WHEN YOUR DIFFERENT.
NOBODY CAN NEVER SAY YOU
COPIED. BE UNIQUE, BE YOU.

YOU CAN BE WHATEVER YOU
WANT TO BE. BUT IT STARTS
WITH YOU. IN ORDER TO BE
THE PERSON YOU DREAM OF,
YOU HAVE TO GO OUT THERE
AND WORK FOR IT. HUSTLE
HARD, DON'T BE A RETARD.
ITS ALL UP TO YOU. YOU GOT
THIS.

WE ALL FALL SHORT. BEST PART
OF FALLING SHORT, IS PICKING
YOURSELF BACK UP.

CONQUEROR

Rejection push me harder,
Pain made me wiser,
Betrayal opened my eyes clearer,
Shame leaned me towards God quicker.
Through, all of the trials I've been through,
My eyes was still stuck on God like clue,
Half the times I didn't know what I was going through.
But my Faith got me stronger than my past,
God got me not trying to go back.
I was really on the wrong track.
Yet,
God always had my back.
Yeap it's time to move forward without looking back.
I know it's not gone be easy,
But I'm ready to be free at last.
From the Fighting,
Fussing,
Drama
And the Karma.
So I gotta say peace to the streets,
Cause I realize,
It's only me,
I hope you feeling me.

VERY MISUNDERSTOOD. AND I REALLY DON'T CARE FOR NO'ONE TO UNDERSTAND ME.

GUARD YOUR THOUGHTS. DON'T LET THE DOUBTS, DISCOURAGE YOU.

STEP OUT ON FAITH AND FOLLOW YOUR DREAMS. TAKE RISK, YOU NEVER KNOW WHAT YOU ARE CAPABLE OF UNTIL YOU TAKE A STEP.

BEING SUCCESSFUL TAKES TIME AND DEDICATION. IT ISN'T A EASY JOB. BUT WITH FOCUS. DETERMINATION AND DESIRE. YOU WILL BE SUCCESSFUL. CONTINUE REACHING TOWARDS THE MOUTAINS.

HERE'S A SMILE FOR THOSE THAT'S FEELING DOWN. REMEMBER YOU WON'T STAY DOWN FOREVER. THERE'S A TOMORROW.

IN LOVING MEMORY OF STUDDA

They say it was a drive by
But why did STUDDA have to die
She was only 18, she wasn't even mean
She stayed clean
Now she got the whole city
Feeling like it's just a dream.
Her whole team, came together as a family.
Nobody was left out.
That's how she would've wanted it to be.
Dang, this really hit home team.
Got her mama and family screaming like "how could this be".
Saying she didn't deserve what just happened to STUDDA.
They took away a daughter, a sister, a friend even took someone's girlfriend who she claim to love forever.
Man everybody crying,
Feeling like their dying, cause when they took you they took a big part of the community.
That was so mean, driving by shooting and hitting the lil homie.
Got everybody going crazy,
But God had a better place for her to be.
So wipe y'all tears cause she up in heaven becoming the angel y'all never thought she was gone be.

DECLARE EVERYTHING IN THE ATMOSPHERE. STAND STRONG AND HAVE FAITH THAT EVERYTHING IS COMING TO PASS.

YOU GOTTA BELIEVE, ONLY WAY THINGS WILL COME TO PASS. TRUST THE PROCESS, EVERY STEP OF IT.

EACH DAY WE HAVE AN OPTION TO CHANGE OR STAY THE SAME. CHOOSE WISELY.

NEVER BE AFRAID TO PRAISE GOD. HE IS THE MASTER OF OUR UNIVERSE. HE REWARDS THOSE WHO AREN'T AFRAID TO TELL THE WORLD WHAT HE HAS DONE THEM.

AGREE WITH GOD, DEPEND ON GOD, TRUST IN GOD AND MOST OF ALL HAVE FAITH IN GOD. YOUR CURRENT SITUATION ISN'T THE END OF YOUR JOURNEY.

ABOUT THE AUTHOR

Maj D., is a Haitian American, born in Miami, Florida. She now resides in Atlanta, Georgia.
She discovered her talent was writing in 2015. When she wrote her first poem and recorded it. She then post it on social media, where she received a numerous amount of Praise. #SpeakFreely is her second collection of self-published work.

Made in the USA
Lexington, KY
15 September 2018